GRAPHIC LIBRARY™

INVENTIONS AND DISCOVERY

LEVI STRAUSS
AND BLUE JEANS

by Nathan Olson

illustrated by Dave Hoover, Keith Williams,
and Charles Barnett III

Consultant:
John Mark Lambertson
Director and Archivist
National Frontier Trails Museum
Independence, Missouri

Capstone
press

Mankato, Minnesota

Graphic Library is published by Capstone Press,
151 Good Counsel Drive, P.O. Box 669, Mankato, Minnesota 56002.
www.capstonepress.com

1 2 3 4 5 6 11 10 09 08 07 06

Library of Congress Cataloging-in-Publication Data
Olson, Nathan.
    Levi Strauss and blue jeans / by Nathan Olson ; illustrated by Dave Hoover, Keith Williams,
and Charles Barnett III.
    p. cm.—(Graphic library. Inventions and discovery)
    Includes bibliographical references and index.
    ISBN-13: 978-0-7368-6484-8 (hardcover)
    ISBN-10: 0-7368-6484-9 (hardcover)
    ISBN-13: 978-0-7368-9646-7 (softcover pbk.)
    ISBN-10: 0-7368-9646-5 (softcover pbk.)
    1. Strauss, Levi, 1829–1902—Juvenile literature. 2. Levi Strauss and Company—History
—Juvenile literature. 3. Jeans (Clothing)—California—History—Juvenile literature. 4. Jeans
(Clothing)—California—History—Comic books, strips, etc. I. Hoover, Dave, 1955– II. Williams,
Keith, 1958 Feb. 24– III. Barnett, Charles, III. IV. Title. V. Series.
HD9940.U4S7974 2007
338.7'687113092—dc22   2006008310

Summary: In graphic novel format, tells the story of Levi Strauss and the evolution of blue jeans.

Art Direction and Design
Bob Lentz

Colorist
Matt Webb

Editor
Donald Lemke

TABLE OF CONTENTS

CHAPTER 1
Gold Fever

In January 1848, a man worked at Sutter's Mill near San Francisco, California. He was about to make a discovery that would forever change the United States of America.

This little rock is mighty shiny. Can it be?

Is this GOLD?!

Soon, Americans were eager to go to California for the chance to strike it rich.

Peddlers walked many miles each day, often to make pennies from their sales. At night, they slept in barns or outdoors.

I wish father could see me now. I carry a peddler's pack just like he did in Bavaria.

It's honest work. I think he would be proud of me.

Levi's family left Germany after his father died. Like other immigrants, the Strauss family came looking for a better life in America.

In Bavaria, they say the streets in America are paved with gold. Maybe in California that's true.

I should go to find out for myself. I can sell goods in California as well as anywhere else.

15

17

Business continued to be very good at Levi Strauss & Company. In July 1872, Levi got a letter with a great idea for his pants.

This is an interesting letter, Fanny. I think we can make the waist-high overalls even better.

You're never satisfied with your own success, are you, brother?

CHAPTER 4

Big Business

Levi's waist-high overalls eventually became known as Levi's denim jeans. The man who's name meant durable, long-lasting clothing was proud that hard-working people everywhere wore Levi's.

Cowboys herding cattle across the Great Plains found that Levi's wore well even after months in the saddle.

Railroad workers laying track east and west across the United States wore their Levi's for years.

Farmers from coast to coast, growing crops to feed a growing nation, worked from dawn to dusk in Levi's.

In 1936, more than 30 years after Levi's death, the red tab label was added to Levi's jeans.

Together with the orange "V" stitching and the leather patch, these trademarks can still be found on every pair of 501 jeans made by Levi Strauss & Co. today.

MORE ABOUT STRAUSS AND BLUE JEANS

LEVI'S In 1906, a great earthquake struck San Francisco, igniting fires that destroyed much of the city. Historical records for Levi Strauss & Co. were destroyed. Many details about the life of Levi Strauss are based on legends rather than historical facts. Historians believe the story of Strauss making canvas pants for a gold miner is a myth. Such a legend probably grew from the need for sturdy clothing and the popularity of denim pants with pocket rivets.

LEVI'S Levi Strauss was born Loeb Strauss in Buttenheim, Bavaria, on February 26, 1829. He moved to New York in 1847, and by 1850 he was known as Levi Strauss. At the age of 73, Strauss died on September 26, 1902, in San Francisco, California.

LEVI'S Levi's father, Hirsch Strauss, was a dry goods peddler in Bavaria. His four children with his first wife were Jacob, Jonas, Lippman (later called Louis), and Maila (later called Mary). After his first wife died in 1822, Hirsch married Rebecca Haas. They had two children, Vogela (later called Fanny) and Loeb (later called Levi).

LEVI'S A typical pair of Levi's 501 jeans takes almost 2 yards of denim, 213 yards of thread, five buttons, and six rivets.

Levi's first jeans were made in two styles. One was the dark blue denim. The other was a light-brown material called "duck." This canvaslike material was as sturdy as denim but not as soft and comfortable. Eventually, Levi stopped making pants out of duck and only used denim for jeans.

One bolt of denim weighs about a quarter of a ton. Cutters use an electric saw to cut through 120 layers of cloth at one time. About 60 pairs of jeans can be cut from one bolt of fabric.

Rivets in the rear pockets of Levi's were covered beginning in 1937. People complained that the rivets scratched school desk chairs and horse saddles. In 1966, reinforced stitching replaced the back pocket rivets on Levi's.

GLOSSARY

canvas (KAN-vuhss)—a type of coarse, strong cloth used for tents, sails, and clothing

denim (DEN-im)—strong cotton material used to make jeans and other articles of clothing

patent (PAT-uhnt)—a legal document giving someone sole rights to manufacture or sell a product

rivet (RIV-it)—a strong metal bolt that is used to fasten something together

trademark (TRADE-mark)—a symbol that shows that a product is made by a particular company

INTERNET SITES

FactHound offers a safe, fun way to find Internet sites related to this book. All of the sites on FactHound have been researched by our staff.

Here's how:
1. Visit *www.facthound.com*
2. Choose your grade level.
3. Type in this book ID **0736864849** for age-appropriate sites. You may also browse subjects by clicking on letters, or by clicking on pictures and words.
4. Click on the **Fetch It** button.

FactHound will fetch the best sites for you!

READ MORE

Blashfield, Jean F. *The California Gold Rush.* We the People. Minneapolis: Compass Point Books, 2001.

Doeden, Matt. *John Sutter and the California Gold Rush.* Graphic Library. Mankato, Minn.: Capstone Press, 2006.

Ford, Carin T. *Levi Strauss: The Man Behind Blue Jeans.* Famous Inventors. Berkley Heights, N.J.: Enslow, 2004.

Peterson, Tiffany. *Levi Strauss.* Lives and Times. Chicago: Heineman Library, 2003.

Raatma, Lucia. *Levi Strauss.* Early Biographies. Minneapolis: Compass Point Books, 2004.

BIBLIOGRAPHY

Cray, Ed. *Levi's.* Boston: Houghton Mifflin, 1978.

Downey, Lynn. "Invention of Levi's 501 Jeans." Levi Strauss & Co. http://www.levistrauss.com/about/history/jeans.htm

INDEX